O PARADISE

O PARADISE

poems by William Trowbridge

THE UNIVERSITY OF ARKANSAS PRESS

FAYETTEVILLE • 1995

99 98 97 96 95   5 4 3 2 1

Designed by Ellen Beeler

♾ The paper used in this publication meets the minimum requirements of the
American National Standard for Permanence of Paper for Printed Library
Materials Z39.48-1984.

Library of Congress Cataloging-in-Publication Data

Trowbridge, William, 1941–
    O paradise / William Trowbridge.
        p. cm.
    ISBN 1-55728-341-9 (cloth). — ISBN 1-55728-342-7 (pbk.)
    I. Title.
PS3570.R6602 1995
811'.54—dc20   94-32342
                                                            CIP

Front jacket/cover illustration by Alice Upham Smith

For Jennifer, Sean, and Randall

ACKNOWLEDGMENTS

Thanks are due to the editors of the following periodicals in whose pages these poems first appeared: *Black Warrior Review:* "Shoah," "The Kiss," "Million Dollar Winners"; *The Chariton Review:* "Snafu," "The Lewis Chessmen"; *Colorado Review:* "Why Astaire," "Phantom Sleep"; *The Georgia Review:* "Great Big Crybabies," "Saint's Life," "O Paradise," "Missing Person" "Interstate"; *The Gettysburg Review:* "Flashbacks," "Foxfire"; *The Journal:* "The Armor of Henry VIII," "That'll Be the Day," "Urn Burial"; *Light:* "Faith"; *The Louisville Review:* "Doctor's Appointment"; *New Letters:* "American Gothic," "In My Father's Buick," "Prayer," "'Rosebud'"; *Pivot:* "Queer Street," "Fall Weather," "Encounter at an Out-of-Town Bar"; *Poet & Critic:* "Mort the Dork," "Kong Views an Experimental Art Film at the City Library"; *Poetry:* "Sometimes on the Porch in Summer," "Living with Solar Keratosis"; *Prairie Schooner:* "Hope"; *Sandscript:* "At My Wife's Family Reunion"; *Shenandoah:* "Scot-Free"; *Spoon River Quarterly:* "Slug," "Libraries," "Break," *Tar River Poetry:* "The Dead," "Little Boy," "Endangered Species," "Bad Birds," "Cinema Des Beaux Arts," "Dump Rats"; *Zone 3:* "Walk, Don't Run," "Valediction Explaining Divorce," "The Farewell of William S. Hart".

My sincerest thanks also to Robert Wallace, Jonathan Holden, Jim Simmerman, Randall Freisinger, and David Slater, friends who lent their time and expertise to help in the making of this book. And thanks to the Corporation of Yaddo, the MacDowell Colony, and the Ragdale Foundation, at whose accommodations much of it was written.

CONTENTS

One

Two

Three

ONE

QUEER STREET

is where they said LaMotta got waylaid
when he stopped that uppercut from Sugar Ray
and kept on standing, or where Basilio wandered
when, once more, his delicate eyes puffed
into two large eggs cooked over easy. It's there
we find ourselves when the playground bully
springs our clock or the green-gowned medico
says breathe deep and count to ten. By five
it's Queer Street, that titled byway
through Palookaville, that rambling road
between this world and the next, which doesn't
look as if it leads to anywhere important,
bliss or opposite. Its few dim bulbs
flicker behind the copper-tasting haze,
and there we stand, befuddled and alone, feeling
more like the village idiot than a traveler
with one foot in the absolute. Quite disappointing,
really, if we had the sense to think so.

FLASHBACKS

They descend and lift us away from what's
at hand as if it didn't really count, as if
getting to sleep or paying the orthodontist
or making sure the coffee pot's unplugged
were just as shadowy as what's rolled off
behind us like something in a rearview mirror.
We're Dorothy watching the fragments of our lives
sail Ozward three miles over Wichita
—there's the old blue bug convertible,
new and poised for that impulse trip
to Mazatlan; there's Clipper,
dead twelve years, finishing
an evening pee; then, single file:
Gramps in Stetson, our whitewalled Schwinn
skidding sideways on gravel, the sewer scent
of L Street after rain, a breezy twilight
on the elm-lined cul-de-sac
that circles past our true love's window,
where our heart unfurls its small sails.

Shortly, we're dropped back onto Kansas,
our flesh recalling the shiver of non-entity,
the exquisite sweep of thin air.

.

INTERSTATE

(I-35 North, Iowa)

The last thing you remember seeing: that billboard
advertising advertising on a rise just past
the Swaledale turnoff; now the sign
reads MASON CITY NEXT 2 EXITS,
patches of old snow melting on the shoulders.
A Perkins, a Wendy's. How long have you been missing?
Ten miles? Twenty? And how'd you do it, with your family
right there thinking something more
than protoplasm steered them around the curves
and slowpokes? Are they so accustomed to your lack
by now that you can disappear unnoticed
—no wires, mirrors—before their very eyes?
Or, did they, too, drift beyond the car, afterwards
solely occupied by soulless ones
or ones with souls suspended and displaced
by, who knows, some ectoplasmic hitchhikers
hopping easy as you please from car to car
on their way to this year's International
Convocation of the Dead, in Winnipeg?
And when your ghost slipped out of Iowa, what

was your state? Weltschmerz? Ennui?
Or simply southern Minnesota, your haste
to reach the Clinic whisking you ahead to Rochester?
Maybe you died and went to heaven, only
to be dropped back here, on cruise control,
hoping the doctors can scope out just
what makes *you* worry so, when *everybody's*
passing through those walls to someplace else,
turning Jacob Marley or Ulalume
and back twenty, fifty times a week,
a day. Who's got time to count? Besides
here's Northwood, twenty miles past Mason City.

"ROSEBUD"

And right before the glass globe tumbles,
smashing beside our bed, spilling water,
fake snowflakes, the little blind chalet
across the floor, what will drift into
that room inside our head, where almost everything's
been repossessed, to be the last fragment
of this life we'll have the chance to kiss
good-bye? Something humble, you can bet,
what with all our more important and presentable
occasions—commencement, marriage, promotion—doing
lunch with their newer, more affluent clientele.
Probably something sad as well, like Charles'
wooden sled, which the movers burned with all
the other junk; something we treasured once,
if only for an afternoon we couldn't recall
now for that million bucks we've heard about.

Sometimes something sits us up in bed
at 3 A.M. and we have to touch our face
to see if we're alive, it feels so close. It's
nothing. Meanwhile we watch the final scene
again, where the rosebud wrinkles up in flames,
which makes us feel like a disappointed ghost
killing time in a theater for ghosts, who lean
across us, nodding their airy heads. "That's
exactly what it's like," they concur. "So real!"

SCOT-FREE

"Go on, beat it," smiles the cop in *Mildred Pierce,*
a moustached vet with a heart the size of Paramount,
and we feel the tug again, as if it's us,
not her, who's been handed yet another pass
through Hell-to-Pay.
                              It *is* us, back
at the candy counter, the electric shock
of getting nabbed still tingling on our cheeks,
Mr. Perkins, who goes to our parents' church,
bending over us in mid-decision, letting
the filched Butterfinger dangle in his hand
like a nightstick. Then: "Go on, beat it,"
and the cool rinse of release.
                              We beat it fast,
still do, when the blood tests come back
negative, when the car stops spinning
on the icy bridge, when the call that wakes us
at 3 A.M. is someone ordering Chinese food.

SNAFU

Sometimes you hear about another one:
the housewife who checked the gas tank
with her lighter, the outlaw sprinting
from the lynch mob, his twin revolvers drawn,
who wound up shooting himself in *both* feet,
the troubadour crushed beneath a balcony
by a falling pig. Some make their own
hard knocks, some attract them like mice
do bull snakes. I knew a guy in high school
named Ralph. "You won't believe what they did
to Ralph," I'd hear, believing already.
Whatever the case, we're supposed to laugh,
and we usually do, they seem so outlandish,
like Job done up in nose and baggy pants,
yet underneath, we sense, so like ourselves,
expelled from youth, sold a cottage
on this marshy landfill, forgetting our car keys
and, eventually, our car—four legs,
two legs, three legs, none—time's schlemiels
sizzling down our length of rope. So we laugh,
sometimes as if our luck depended on it.

THE KISS

(V-J Day, Times Square, 1945)

Famous and faceless as those who raised
the flag on Suribachi, they lean forever
in black and white: the randy gob, fresh
from sailing back alive, who's just found
something better to kiss than pavement,
and the nurse whose sheer-white-stockinged legs
show trim as any pin-up girl's.
Bent backward and off balance in his arms,
she catches what he's found the nerve to pitch,
her right knee bending slightly
from his boyish ardor. Passers-by await
the finish, poised to applaud or cheer,
but the two go on and on, picked up by *Life*
to show us what we fight for. Are they lovers?
Strangers? Is the whole thing being posed
for the Sunday supplement?
                                                    We cannot know.
The show ends here, as did our latest dance
to death's slick croon, with the kind of kiss

that Bogart planted on Bacall. The rest,
as we're sometimes told, belongs to history,
off camera, clearing its rheumy throat.

CINEMA DES BEAUX ARTS

About us with firepower they were never wrong,
the old comedians: how well they understood
the imbecility; how we so often mistake
the quick fuse for the slow, or get chased down
by our own lonely rockets, or, aiming for the grouse,
crease the warden's behind; how, while adults
are reverently, hilariously blazing away,
there must never be children in the scene,
most of whom would pray for it not to happen.
They never forgot
that even the keeper of the most dreadful weapon
can end up, anyway, in some untidy situation,
the errant fireball hoisting him to kingdom come,
which, in his case, is hot year-round and very noisy.

In Keaton's *The General,* for instance, how everything
consents quite leisurely to the blundering: Buster
loads a giant siege mortar, mounted
on a rolling flat car, with enough black powder

for a moon shot, then lights the fuse and runs back
to the engine cab, after which vibration lifts the barrel,
rotates it over till it points straight at our hero.
For him, it was an important failure, worse
when he hooked his foot trying to uncouple the car.
We were about to see something amazing—a man
completely perforating himself with a bowling ball—
when the train puffed calmly around a bend and,
no thanks to the dour-browed human looking on,
the innocent ball sailed into a stand of poplars.

WALK, DON'T RUN

(To a Japanese Soldier Burned Alive on Saipan)

Maybe you'd heard it, too, back in school:
that feeble bromide for when the bulldog
charges or the bully strides behind you,
stepping on your heels. Walk briskly and they'll
break off, acquiesce, think they mistook you
for someone else; or maybe they'll just
lose track as you blend in with the world's
supply of walkers, like Dr. Richard Kimball,
The Fugitive, who stayed on the run by walking soft,
or Peter, hoping nature wouldn't recognize
the breach as he wobbled across the waves
to Jesus. Or the hobblers and the weavers
on their morning laps inside the mall,
trying to keep a step on what's begun
to shadow them. Maybe that's what you were doing
when, ablaze, you took those four unearthly steps
past the foe outside your smoldering bunker,
then crumbled to your knees and dropped
face down, blending in, beyond recognition.

SHOAH

*After the war, we read masses of accounts of the ghettos and the extermi-
nation camps, and we were devastated. But when we see today Claude
Lanzmann's extraordinary film, we realize we have understood
nothing. . . . Now, for the first time, we live it in our minds, and
hearts and flesh. It becomes our experience.*
—SIMONE DE BEAUVOIR

I'm in for the whole nine hours of talking
heads, forest clearings, rolling trains,
what's left of Sobibor, Auschwitz, Treblinka.
Now it's Abraham Bomba, retired barber
coaxed back to his shop in Tel-Aviv,
told to keep cutting on a well-coifed man
who's trying not to look at the camera,
and to tell us how it felt when he first
saw naked women hunched beneath his scissors.
Bomba snips and snips, applying the comb
each time, never looking up, cleaving
to the facts in a flattened voice
that sounds too loud in the silence
of this busy spot for news and gossip:

> *How we did it—cut as fast as we could.*
> *We were quite a number of professional*
> *barbers, and the way we did it, we just*
> *did this and this like this here and*
> *this side and that and the hair was all*
> *finished.*

But Lanzmann, lucky Jew,
passed over by that storm of "Jewish luck,"
as Bomba calls it, won't relent.
And I, not even passed over, not even
remotely Jew, though no less
a lucky Jew for that, urge him on
from my chair. We have to pry this Bomba
loose from his grip on facts, finger
by finger, if we have to break
them all, because we mean to have what
we couldn't get from Mordechai Podchlednik,
who wouldn't stop smiling because,
"Sometimes you smile, sometimes you cry.
And if you're alive, it's better to smile"
or plucky Rudolph Vrba, who said,
"*Laufschritt,* yeah, never walking
—everything had to be done in *laufschritt,*
immer laufen. So, very sporty—they
were a sporty nation, you see" or from

Simon Srebnik or Paula Biren or Filip
Muller or Gertrude Schneider and
her mother or the villagers at Chelmno
and Belzec or from the dollhouse model
of Krematorium II, which looked like
an International House of Pancakes
with a large square chimney: the dolls
led in, the dolls undressing, the dolls
piled halfway to the ceiling. "Dolls,"
said Motke Zaidl, "the Germans made us
call the bodies *Figuren,* that is,
puppets, dolls, —or *Schmattes,*
which means 'rags.'"

　　　　　　We've got to get it straight
Lanzmann and me, to corner it and grasp it
with our minds, our hearts, our lucky flesh,
here, now, beyond its brimstone-stinking forests,
in the ordinary sunlight of a shave and trim,

and so it's Abraham Bomba, starting to lose
his grip, down to two white fingers,
turning his face away from the camera, which
zooms in as we proceed: "But I asked you
and you didn't answer. How did it feel?"
No fingers now, the facts scattering on the floor:

> *I tell you something . . . . To have*
> *a feeling about that . . . it was very hard*
> *to feel anything, because working there*
> *day and night between dead people, between*
> *bodies, your feeling disappeared, you were*
> *dead, with your feeling. You had no feeling*
> *at all.*

                          Then
he sees them, not the heads lined up,
the piles of hair, the bodies spilling out
like truckloads of potatoes, but just two people,
the wife and sister of a fellow barber

from his village. He's trying to swallow
them, like a cornered agent gagging down
the secret list. He waves us off,
rubs his eyes and forehead with a clean towel,
paces about in dead air rising thick
as Zyklon B. "It's too horrible,
please," he says, and glares at us. But
we insist, we apologize and press him till
he coughs them up, the wife, the sister,
though not in time. Nothing's left
but two blue figures, small and flat
as paper dolls, and the thrum of traffic
on the sunny street outside.

THE ARMOR OF HENRY VIII

The White Tower, London

Two of his abandoned shells
ignore each other in their separate
glassed displays. Hogging front and center,
the bloated Piltdown, arms akimbo,
jaw thrust out, buckles strained
across a huge round ass and gouty
legs, codpiece loud as a Buick hubcap.
This one knows what he's entitled to
and means to bolt it anaconda style,
his conscience now the Church
where smart men worship every day.

Back by a window dreams the forgotten
novice, hands on pike, alert
and lean, tilted forward as if he sees
something amazing moving in
from the distance: a bookish vision
of Britannia with a ring, or, in that bright
disguise, her opposite, some swollen thing
about to meet its match.

BULK MAIL

All young people appear to be
suspect—and so liable to
"Disappearance"—in areas where
the guerillas are active.
— AMNESTY INTERNATIONAL

Today in Ayacucho, the square
abounds with snapshots
of the disappeared: sweepstakes
entries, though the deadline's passed.
In the mail today, I find
the winners: nine lucky
faces chosen for a postcard.
Millions will see them
in their best clothes and most
serious smiles, yet somehow
tentative as spirits at a seance.
Overexposed, five have barely
made the trip, one
little more than an outline
with hair and blouse, like an ad
to "Draw the Girl." I'd give
her back eyes, lips, nose
before she bleeds completely
into light, a glossy

blankness creased and smudged
from carrying. She'd be lucky
as the rest, famous in America.

THE LEWIS CHESSMEN

*(a twelfth-century set of humorously carved figures discovered
in 1831 on the Isle of Lewis)*

Some seven centuries beyond their models
and their maker, these mumpish, boss-eyed gnomes
stare, not at us, but at something that's got
the King's dander up, the Queen's right hand
pressed against her cheek. The Bishop holds
his two-fingered blessing close to his cassock,
while the Knight glowers from a qualmish little horsie
and the fuming Warder chomps down hard
on the top of his shield. "No laughing matter,"
they concur. "Something's rotten in the parish of Uig."

Rotten indeed, to prompt this royal dudgeon,
fixed for keeps in walrus tusk: the pawns,
perhaps, with their clownish disrespect for mace
and miter, who had no better sense than to pose
decked out as two squat rows of tombstones.

THE AMERICAN SCHOLAR
MEETS THE TOAD WORK

He sees a bushel and his cart and nothing beyond, and sinks into the
farmer, instead of Man on the Farm.
    —EMERSON

Work, alas, must have its toad-hearted
sway down every blessed furrow and back.
"I'll be the symbol here," it croaks, squatting
beneath a bush where the sun can't reach.
"Go break some sod before I transfer you
to spreading shit or, better yet, pack
you off to stand for Man Without Employment!"

Its regimen's not all bad, though, paying the bills
and, more important, nagging us to see
the human alphabet in lower case—
farmer, felon, friend, foe, flunkie—
locking up those sacramental robes
of craven Thisness or pardon-my-magnificence
Thatness which cover up our homely gait
and make us seem to glide on air or brimstone,
mark us for staterooms or the high speed oven.

MORT THE DORK

Remember death in seventh grade? The runt
afraid to take a shower, the easy out,
the one who couldn't tag his ass in Kick the Can,
whose bawling in the dirt clod fights
signaled time to run for home, and then,
when there were girls, the chess club's
glum and solitary member, its founding
his only credit in the yearbook, where he's listed
under "Not Pictured." And later, in his absence
at reunions, the boozy tales of how he drifted
into business school, passed every course
through sheer staying power till he found
his knack for acquisition, trading up
and up till now he's got a hold on almost
everything, of how he's conquered sleep,
of how he remembers *all* his old classmates.

LETTER TO
AETHELRED THE UNREADY

> *. . . and the king was sent to in London; they bade him come to meet the troops with all the aid he could gather. When they all came together, it availed no more than it ever had.*
> —1016 A.D., *THE ANGLO-SAXON CHRONICLES*

Somehow it's *your* moldy cloak that fits us
right off the rack. Not straight like William's or broad
like Harry's, its plain Republican shoulders hold
the shape of your final shrug when Cnut and the Cnutites
stir-fried Cornwall for the umpteenth time,
having blown your latest tribute, as usual, on enormous,
woolly appetites. Nothing left to throw them
but the towel of state—clergy, thanes, and churls
already thumbing through their phrase books: "Hey,
Oly, you like art prints? Kiss, kiss?"

We know, we know: unready but hardly, by then,
surprised—"This doesn't surprise me in the least!"
you must have announced to bare walls after Mrs.
Aethelred, turned Clairol blonde, took off for Olso
behind a Hitler Youth, the two of them mounted
on your best white charger, still under warranty.

VALEDICTION EXPLAINING DIVORCE

Suppose, just because
nobody's found the answer
page on this one,
that when two souls
become one,
one of the lovers
is then short a soul,
that the hungrier gets
both, which are now
only one,
and, because souls
are, by definition,
incorporeal and,
according to most
experts, undifferentiated,
the lucky recipient
isn't a nickel
better off than before
—so that each party

begins to feel like someone
whose wallet's just been
lifted, a suspicion which,
in time, gives pause,
followed by thoughts
of new and altogether
separate personal growth
experiences, which,
after the appropriate
vituperation and legal
fees, produce a document
both petitioners (hereafter
the parties of the first
part and of the second
part) see as page one
of a rich and creative life
script, later to seem
more like the butt end
of a pyramid scheme.

SLUG

Silent as time, simple as snot,
I make my rounds among leaves and stems,
going in moonlight, morose and gray,
phlegmatic locomotion beneath your view.

Naked membrane, a meal for crows,
stomach-foot on a trail of slime,
ancient, limber, I ooze along
munching my way through your bed of roses.

I leave you notes in a rainbow film,
a drunk unraveling of loamy love
that's blind and patient, cold and moist,
dark as the dreams you don't remember.

FAITH

(as Boeing 747)

Each, in turn, ignores the scoffs, lumbers
its tonnage down the slabs toward cyclone fence
and holocaust in crowded shopping mall,
then heaves its mammoth ass into nothing
but thin air, and (the mustard-seed surprise)
rarely drops like fifteen-story buildings
should, but shrinks itself to goose. And flies.

GREAT BIG CRYBABIES

Once, we could do it over gumballs,
half asleep: the sweet boohoo or commanding
howl we mastered on the first try, straight
from the womb—our delivery so cute, so nubby,
so coochie-coo and dimpled, they almost *had* to
fetch us what we wanted or less of what
we didn't want. Sometimes they'd send Dad
running for the camera.
                              But we've lost our touch,
like the pitcher who sees his killer fast ball
climbing toward the upper deck in center,
or the Wall Street *Wunderkind* whose golden goose
reverts to goose eggs.
                              Now some Quasimodo
grown from our former selves shakes the bed in winter
and rises to clutch some fragment from an old
foreclosure: monarchs drowsy in a stand of milkweed,
or the tug of three bright half-notes drifting
from an open window. "Whungh!" he utters.

"What was *that* about?" we ask ourselves
the next day at the bathroom mirror. But back there,
barefoot in the dark kitchen, it's "Whungh! Hoo-boo!"

TWO

WHY ASTAIRE

Because he could take what twists our ankles, scrapes
our knees, cuts our fingers, what strains, bloodies,
chips, barks, and fractures—all the world's
impedimenta—and teach it how to dance
with him, of all people; those outsized hands
and feet, the whole frame, like ours, unlikely,
not cut out for looking debonair.

Yet chairs rumbaed, brooms sambaed, canes
were coaxed into the carioca. His adagio
with clothes tree, for example, where he sweeps
inertia off its legs, breezing through the rudiments
of glide and leap and pirouette till dead wood
waits on edge for his return
to catch it in mid-swoon and, finally, waltz it
around to its customary spot. When the lights
go up, we sigh into ourselves, rise
for our occasions, thinking *These hands, these feet.*

AMERICAN GOTHIC

When methane breaches
in a septic tank
it says, "Bleak," the word
we like best. Make ours
bleak. Easy on the salt
and garnish: we want it gray
on a gray dish. And let it
sit for a while,
like leftovers.

And give us a bleak place
to eat it: wood frame,
dim inside, even
at high noon—heavy
drapes and wall-to-wall
linoleum. The siding
we want grit-gray,
with maybe a tinge of rust
leaching through. Sky

and ground the color
of erasures. We
like it that way.

What we don't like
is interruptions,
which is why
we keep our guns
where we can get
our hands on them
and why we take black-
and-white photos
of strangers. We make
no exceptions, not even
for you. Why should we?
Even now, you're
interrupting. Maybe
people where you
come from *like*

that necktie
you've got on.
Read our lips:

Bleak.

MILLION DOLLAR WINNERS

Maybe they're all from one big family:
the Dowdens, Earl and Edna May
or Bud and Doris or Geraldine or Cleon,
dumb luck's baffled elect
gripping an edge of that bed-sized check
from Reader's Digest or Lotto America,
their smiles tight as Earl's new shoes.
We know his answers by heart: he feels
great, he'll retire first thing Monday,
burn the mortgage, spend a whole month
in Vegas or Disney World. We wonder
if *our* dreams would turn so flat
and puny under light. Behind him
in a flowered smock, Edna May stares
past the cameras as if suspecting
something: that we're a tough house
to play, that they'll have to smile
till their faces ache, explain themselves
to us like vacationers whose Winnebago's
stalled in the luckless heart of Newark.

THE GAG

Here's the setup: Gleason as the Poor Soul,
kind of a sadsack Pillsbury Doughboy, lands a job
putting cream pies into boxes as they arrive
on a conveyer belt through a hole in the wall
of an empty white room—pick up pie, box it,
stack it, next pie. Simple enough, but where
are the other workers? and why no labels
on the boxes? Did he see something like this
on *Candid Camera?* Anyway, he pitches in.
And he does OK. He likes the friendly
predictability, the bakery smell, how the clean
white apron feels as the pies line up
like little troopers. The "Washington Post
March" fans out from the back of his scalp
to his forehead and hands; the command
"eyes right" comes to mind. When he looks
in that direction, the conveyer belt's
little electric motors whisper
"Vocation." Maybe he could learn to drive,

buy his clothes at a big men's store, get
married. His jowels feel like they're
firming, growing angular. Only
here's the thing: the belt speeds up,
—not much at first, so he thinks it's just
a momentary lapse of concentration, a result
of overconfidence. So he focuses, tries
to think at least two pies ahead, and things
go back in sync, though there's this pressure
now. Then the belt goes even faster. This time
the pies start backing up. He has to switch
techniques: try to box one pie with his right hand
while he blocks the rest with his left. Sweat's
getting in his eyes and on his apron. If there's
a stop button, nobody told *him* about it. When he
drops his first pie, you see this little squint
of recognition. But there's no time to stop
and figure out what's suddenly so damned
familiar about all this: the pies are climbing up

on each other like sex-crazed turtles.
Some begin to slide off onto the floor,
one landing square on his shoes, as if somebody
actually aimed it, and splurting
up his pantleg. That's it! He does the Poor Soul
take: a mockup of that bitsy cherub mope
that used to make the grown-ups deliver an
"Awwwwww." But there's a big difference
between baby fat and fat fat, and besides,
this system operates by the bottom line,
which is that the pies are now being
catapulted into the wall behind him, splattering
like a swarm of locusts on a windshield,
while the Poor Soul dodges right,
then left, and his fat-boy hands try
to hide inside each other. But now look: the belt's
slowed back to normal, and here comes
the foreman. The Poor Soul tries to explain,
demonstrate, but he can barely

work his arms, and the electric motors,
their bearings shot, drown him out
with a smoky yammering. He gets the quick
heave-ho, shuffling his sorry dough legs
out the back door. As we have a good laugh,
the theme, played by Miami Beach's own
Sammy Spear and his famous orchestra,
rises in our fat-boy throats.

THE DEAD

They like it quiet,
slow-paced, no renters. Some
have practiced all their lives
for this, sitting stone still
at their desks, nodding
off in the BarcaLounger
after the network news. Nothing
could possibly be further
from their loamy minds than a call
to resurrection. They're tired of hearing,
of seeing, of trying to carry on
a halfway decent conversation.
They keep their noses turned up,
even at the smell of fresh coffee.
And they don't take kindly
to square-peg types. Once a vampire
got transferred here by mistake,
complete with fifteen brides
right out of a Frederick's catalogue

and a record as long as your arm.
The family trade went down
the toilet; even the police
steered clear, till the block committee
paid a call. He sold low
to the judge's daughter, a plain woman
who sleeps with the porch light on.

THE FAREWELL OF WILLIAM S. HART

(a short subject filmed in 1946)

Dug up tonight for a spot on *Cowboy Classics*
between *Geronimo* and Pre-Owned Car of the Week,
the horse-faced hero who scowled above his Colts
through a thousand mute and jerky shootouts, steps
before us hatless and disarmed, breaks the silence
with a shaking, Thespian voice, eyes reflecting
a plea that, somehow, sincerity and passion
count for something in the end, perhaps enough
to push aside Autry, Rogers, and the other dudes
strumming beside their halfwit toadies
and summon everything back, if only
for a few more runs: those rushing afternoons
he struggles here to make us see, when he rode
back from the day's last chase, hearing
the director's voice, alone and faraway
as his now sounds as he turns to find
himself cantering in from the horizon and calls,
"THAT   WAS   O   K,   BILL.   THAT'S   A   TAKE."

"Oh, the *thrill* of it," he mourns, turning back
to us with a look that knows how little
he's asking, really, what a harmless switch
in time's million-reeler: Bill Hart
back at the canteen in blousy neckerchief
and scoutmaster hat, six-guns puffing
silence at the foe's bubonic heart. I want
to stand up and go corny, to wave a Stetson
high enough for him to spot across half
a century, to holler, as the evening sun ignites
his cloud of dust, "GOOD   LUCK,   BILL.
GIVE 'EM   ONE   FOR YOUR OLD   SADDLE   PALS."

THAT'LL BE THE DAY

February 3, 1959

The morning news
showed no bodies,
no medics in white,
no gawkers jostling
with camera crews:
only four men
in hats and overcoats,
standing with arms hung down
by a snowy cornfield
and staring past
a bale-sized fist
of metal stopped
against a barbed-wire fence.
Like a stray cow,
an old Caddy ambulance
idled at the roadside.

It might have been a false alarm,
though somewhere in the stubble

lay the ones
who dropped unheard
the night before and,
to what must have been their sheer
astonishment, perished
by the simplest laws
of mass and motion,
leaving nothing unsettled
for those sent out
but the day's slow drill
of paperwork and phone calls,
of picking up
and hauling off.

"STRANGE MEADOWLARK"

(on saxophonist Paul Desmond of the Dave Brubeck Quartet)

Aloof on stage, sedate in gray like a frugal
billionaire, removed a step from the band's
half circle, he stands there absent, eyes
closed, hands folded on bell, listening,
not for Brubeck's cue to step back in,
but for something faraway, something the present
riffs and lines are merely filling in for,
to coax him back to modulate the world,
like some strange meadowlark, alone in a field,
whose gold-leaf notes flow into light
and seem to ride a filigree of air,
though they shape the ragged air, bestow its course,
its pace and pitch and utter depth till everything's
on time, yeah, till everything blows cool.

THE SINGER

(on a poetry reading by Etheridge Knight, Chicago, 1985)

A wall-eyed moon above the podium light,
his face reflects the lumps and fissures of a life
imposed by some cosmic hanging judge: war,
dope, prison, and the bigot's unrelenting
stare. Before he says (not "reads," he insists)
his poems, he'll prepare us with a song he has to use
when bad nights crowd him right into the wall,
shove his face against the cinder block
till he wants to get a shank and give them the excuse
they're looking for.
          "Willow, weep for me," he sings,
tremolo on the first surprising note, then smoother:
"Willow, weep for me," and the room wavers,
then dissolves to open night sky, stars
thick and deep as on an ocean, the moon
lifted high above the razor wire, its mouth
an O, its eyes meandering in two directions.

WHAT WE COULD DO

What shall we ever do?
——"THE WASTE LAND"

Late tonight, when Sears or Penney's
or Wal-Mart or even Monkey Ward
wouldn't give us the time of day,
we could dial up L. L. Bean,
bring that voice, bright and infallible
as a tuning fork, into our doubt-strafed,
harshly lighted homes to grant our wish
for a Shepherd's Check Flannel Shirt,
or, if they're out of stock, a pair
of Bolle Irex Aviator Sportglasses,
or, a pair of Helly-Hansen Lifa Prolite
Underwear. We can't afford to be
too choosy, so maybe we could ask *them*
to pick out something nice, a surprise
to lift us from what we call our neighborhood,
that mile-wide miss we still can't quite believe,
and drop us into the shrink-resistant heart
of some coastal woodscape: Look! Down there!
It's our springer spaniel, our teal-green rucksack,
our Easy-Pitch Geodesic Tent with vestibule!

KONG VIEWS AN EXPERIMENTAL
ART FILM AT THE CITY LIBRARY

I sat behind the man in the motorcycle pants
and the woman with hair like a shocked sombrero.
All of us would be blown away in the vast concussion
of Tony's art, which was good. So said the leader,
a tube-shaped woman who made hand washing
motions while recounting Tony's terrible struggle
to get where he was, which was by the cheese plate,
and apologized about the projector's having too little
power for such a large piece of art, though somehow
adjustments were made. And so commenced a mighty
flickering. "FEED ME!" screamed an angry severed
head (Tony's). "CLOTHE ME!" "There is still
PREJUDICE!" Much activity followed this: a person
stood there, another looked aside, another
scratched his foot (all Tony, but with different
earrings each time). Then window curtains parted
to reveal an atomic bomb, Rudy Vallee, and the last
five minutes of someone else's art,
entitled *Easy Rider*. After the applause,

the lights came on, and Tony himself stood
to tell us what to think, though he didn't think
anyone could say anything about what his pictures
meant. "Like meaning," he said, "always means
like the same thing anyway: Bourgeois
Capitalism and Phallocentricity," which I'm
almost sure was that Belgian dance act
I followed at the Roxy. Finally the man
in the pants asked Tony if he didn't think
that the treatment of artists was like the Holocaust
and where did he buy his boots, to which Tony
replied that questions about art were fascist and Gucci's
basement. Before leaving, I tried to drink
some carrot juice out of the little plastic cup.

ENDANGERED SPECIES

So everything's going as usual: "Little pig,
little pig, let me come in." You know the drill.
But this time he opens the door and just
stands there, asking if I've got a permit
for slaughtering animals. I wanna know
since when do wolves need a permit to act
like wolves. Then he asks if I ever
heard of indecent exposure, loitering,
and creating a public nuisance. I'm trying
to figure out whatever happened to "Not
by a hair on my chinny-chin-chin," when
more pigs show up, wearing uniforms
and badges, driving a car with a "Keep America
Clean" bumper sticker. Next thing I know
I'm in the growler with six big boars,
the kind with knives instead of teeth, and tattoos
of naked sows and sayings like "Born
to Root" and "Make Mine Tref." Then one
of them steps up and looks me over with those little

eyes. So I ask him if he ever heard of assault
with a deadly weapon. All he does is grin
and say, "Talk to me, sweet meat."

BAD BIRDS

They swarm in and unpack right
on private property: starlings,
jays, filthy little sparrows. They're not
welcome like our titmice and chickadees
—as if they even care—barging
into the nearest maple or forsythia
with the skree and skrinch of their
nonstop squabbles. Not one
can sing a note, though you'd think
they had an invitation, the way they
slap up nests all over our backyards
and then lay claim to our patios
and sand piles. Our guard dogs
play dead under our sun decks,
refusing to fetch, their poor noses
pecked strawberry. The kids won't
go out anymore. We'd like
to wipe that smirk off Mr. Rodgers'
face, to see Tweetie Bird,

Big Bird, Son-of-a-Bitch Bird
meet Big Wolverine. We have to
get Eyewitness News in fragments
by word-of-mouth. Our down-sized Chevy
wagons are speckled with lime, which
our doctors warn can be dangerous
to our health. Sweet old Mrs. Epley's
papers pile up on her lawn beside
what's left of her favorite Persian. We get
other people's mail, which we
can't make heads or tails of, and even
that has fallen off to a few scraps
we find scattered down
the driveway. Meanwhile, the riffraff
prowl our sidewalks, ruffling
feathers, shouldering squirrels
and tabbies into the street, swelling
bad gene pools with slack-beaked,
serpent-eyed defectives hooked on gum,

cigarette filters, paint chips.
Our application for All-American City
came back stamped "Bad Birds," and the state
police say their hands are tied. We've been
forced to go against our better natures till
we hardly recognize ourselves, toting
propane torches, tennis rackets, scatter
guns—in short, we've had to take
matters into our *own* hands, which hasn't
helped that much because we seem to be
playing into *their* hands: "See?" they tell
our few remaining scarlet tanagers as we
cut loose from inside our circle
of Lawn-Boys. "Who loves you best?"

HOPE

I don't care if they've already won the pennant. They won't beat us again. Pardon the language, but this time, we're not just going to win: we're going to kick their butts.

—ROOKIE FIRST BASEMAN IN A TELEVISION INTERVIEW

Words to eat—but something about the boyish
face, the home team cap set strictly
for business, the factual, born-again tone
leaves me convinced. Baseball bores me stupid,
but I'm going to be there, though I didn't catch
the date or time, didn't even hear who
they are. Down deep, an avuncular voice
approves, says I need to find out, need to
see this. Butt is going to be kicked—
pampered, preening, six-figure butt.
A cocky gang of shoo-ins, primed
for another three-game sweep, is going to chew
something amazing, bitter as ashes,
what our slumping, boozy manager calls
"the breaks" when the flocks of boo birds
waddle in and diehards don their paper bags,
what the numbed tarantula must be tasting
as the wasp prepares him for her brood.

PRAYER

Say a prayer for your pal
on Gaudalcanal.
—WWII GRAFFITO

In case no one ever got around to it,
here goes. I pray that what remains of you
remains upright as a man age . . . what?
. . . seventy-two or so can be, that you didn't
buy it right there among the fronds
and body scraps and maggots, that you walked out
with all your parts whole as a healthy newborn's
and your mind not jammed on perpetual playback,
that afterwards you got a decent draw
in a square house, and that today finds you
shirtless on the patio, a brewski frosting up
beside you, the lawn finished, the double header
about to come on, when all of a sudden a bird
somewhere behind the garage cuts loose
with the most astounding run of notes you think
ever was sung, till your mind skips back
to 1942, the night you crouched
quivering in your foxhole, pissing yourself after
a chunk of shrapnel chimed off your helmet,

thinking how you needed someone's prayer,
an extra voice to maybe boost the odds,
when, off to the left, this bearded fucker with glasses
and a potbelly comes actually flying past,
low and unsteady on fairy wings long
as barge oars, his legs bent gracelessly,
and warbles something, the last part of which
sounded like, you'd swear, "the power of poetry."

SAINT'S LIFE

*Before Joe and Myra were halfway up the stairs, their son was sailing high
over the trees and houses, too amazed to be afraid, and then coasting down
a slow-relaxing ramp of air to land gently in the very center of an empty
block.*
—RUDI BLESH, *KEATON*

Let's face it, classmates, faith's a gift
for being too amazed, too curious
to be afraid when a pasture full of shit
hits the fan, when the huge blind finger
on the horizon finds your house and flicks you out
an upstairs window. Think of little Buster,
windborne, descending like a kite four blocks
away, bemused by Joe and Myra's cries.

Now, when his life flickers miraculously before us,
we fly with him, reel to reel, in a dream of ourselves:
blessed survivors in a world where nothing works,
where everything, sooner or later, breaks, clogs,
goes kerflooey. We show the immortal deadpan,
all staring and cheekbones, as the house falls,
the boat sinks, the Lizzie dies on the tracks,
sure we'll think of something before time runs out
or discover the whole thing's a bluff we can call
by simply standing still: the wall crashes

harmlessly around us, the boat rises on a submarine,
the train switches tracks and blusters off.

Dressed in solemn oaths, our faults and stewings
chase us through the streets, waving their billys,
too fat, too dumb, too choked with rage to ever
beat us to the next corner, the next unreeling,
where the anarchist's bomb serves only to light
our cigarette. The secret is not to break
the face's holy silence, not to laugh,
not even to lift an eyebrow: it gives us away,
spoils the gag, wakes us in midair.

THREE

O PARADISE

Maybe it isn't choirs of cherubim with perfect pitch
or lions snuggling up with lambs and shepherds. Maybe
it's something like a friend and I once saw,
looking in his basement window when we were shy
with zits and stumble bones. There was my friend's
big brother with a girl and his own motorcycle, a candy-apple
Triumph with red-orange flames along the tank and chrome pipes
wide enough for Charlemagne to hear. Yes, there he was,
sitting by the furnace, with girl *and* motorcycle, his hands
dark with gear oil and expertise, and hers the same,
so that if they kissed, and they did, they had to hold
their hands away, as dancers might—a *pas de deaux*
by Kelly and Caron.

> One kiss, then back to bolts
and sprockets for a while; then later, I supposed,
the two of them astride that friendly beast.

> And there
we were, outside, about to pedal into another

Friday night, toward the football game, where cheerleaders
lifted up their arms, which lifted up their breasts,
and kicked the cold October air for love.

DUMP RATS

Unlike the squirrel I shot, who, when the bullet
thumped its life out, sent something back
stringent as the coming on of flu or polio,
they scurried like the Japs on *Victory at Sea,*
jungle-canny, into crevices and holes, behind
new cover faster than your trigger finger,
low-slung, bucktoothed, ruthless as bacteria.

We played our heroes, the Marines, 2nd Division
riflemen dark from Tarawa and Saipan, ready
to flush them out or wait to spot a nose,
a pinkish tail, the polished bead of eye.
Spine shot, they'd sometimes drag in circles,
bite at each new wound.
                              At a cookout
on his screened-in patio, our Scoutmaster,
the drunk Marine, once told us how hara-kiri
looked on Pelalieu, grenade at stomach,
the head snapping back, stomach open,

and one hand gone. Sometimes they'd scurry
down their hole, he said, and then
you'd hear it: boom, boom,   boom.
"A thing like that you never can forget,"
he said, though we didn't want to.

At sunset, our tiny ammo spent,
we'd leave for dinner, flashing a look
or two like the battle-sodden vets in *Life:*
grim-jawed, deep-eyed, omniscient.

LITTLE BOY

Thus was Little Boy engendered,
Thin Man's modest brother . . .
—RICHARD RHODES, *THE MAKING OF THE ATOMIC BOMB*

It was simple science to an eight-year-old
already schooled in fire, electricity,
the abrasiveness of sidewalks and basement stairs:
there, Butchie, the neighbor lady's bulldog,
snoozing by his house, paw on bloody bone,
his blunt hind end presented like a target,
complete with bull's-eye; here, in my hands,
a Daisy carbine, model forty-two,
with the spiffy rawhide thong. Thus, fire A
(particle) into B (bull's-eye) by means of
C (accelerator) to get D (energy, perhaps
as much as I'd observed when Jerry
slipped Tom's tail into an outlet).

So, C fired A dead center into B,
producing an instantaneous mushroom cloud
of D: success, till, shortly afterwards,
the unanticipated fallout E through Z.

HOME FRONT: OMAHA, 1943

Mid-November in a neighborhood
of tilted sidewalks, of bungalows
and thrifty brick apartments,
sunset lush as breaking fever, dampness
bites from roof and chimney shadows
as the five o'clock streetcar sparks
its way from town. Someone's burning
trash before supper, which will consist
of Sunday's shoulder roast with potato
pancakes, all we need, all we want.

Last night, flanked by two MPs, Hope
and Lamour aired the sizzling
of a Porterhouse, a wish
mailed in by a master sergeant
on Tulagi, while the Philco's tubes
glowed a map on our papered wall.

LIBRARIES

I was raised to dodge them as unlucky places,
like museums and cemeteries, granite heavy,
austere, European, vaguely Jewish
though usually feigning Greek. The close air
could dry the tongue, the nostrils, blotting
you down to a pale cicada husk, swept
beneath the unforgiving ranks of shelves,
behind on your book reports till death,
always losing ground, new volumes
springing up like ghetto rats, your eyes
saucered behind the thickening lenses, your mind
bulging dangerously, your sweet, pink heart
flailing like a trapped bird, like little Sir Hugh.

MISS SNIDER

Looming before us in fourth grade history,
too angry to be snide, she became the Inquisition,
Gunboat Diplomacy, Blitzkrieg, the Golden Horde
thundering across the steppes—those Jehovah shoulders,
those sizzling blue wires of hair driving
through bystanders straight for the now-too-late
contrite. Ex-lady-wrestler snatched
nearly bald in back, so the legend
went, she shook us up completely, gripped
window-gazers, snickerers, receivers and concealers
of notes by the upper arms and set herself
on Agitation till brains and eyeballs wobbled
in their cups, then dropped us, seeing double, in our seats.

Drilled on kings, conquistadors, and dates,
we mostly learned how history feels to those
it's written on: Indians singing hymns
in Spanish, pronouncing "free" too loud,
the kid in back storing details for this poem.

IN MY FATHER'S BUICK

This car'll get me
anywhere I want to go.
—HAZEL MOTES

It had Dynaflow: worse than the load of chrome,
the Republican muffler, the family-sized
bulk that cornered like a grain barge,
the push-button windows. Staging for the light
at Twelfth and River, chopped Bel Airs
and raked Fairlanes, their engines wrapped
to bursting, bucked and snarled, jockeying
to shriek away through every blessed gear,
Father, Son, and Holy Ghost
smoking in tandem toward high C,
pressing the girls inside till they gave out
little cries, "Oh." I'd flow behind
in the huff and puff of a fissured boiler,
alone or with my aching friends,
plaguey-faced as Job. At Burger Boy,
between "My Prayer" and "Great Balls
of Fire," the upholstery whispered, "Sophomore.
Second stringer. Snookie Lanson."

One night I took the hubcaps off,
lowered the rear with cinderblocks, tried
popping from Reverse at stop signs. "Dynaflow,"
blabbed the shiny letters on the trunk,
even when I broke 100 through the thick,
wet moonlight outside town. "Dynaflow,"
mouthed the Angels, hanging right beside me,
their red Deuce backing off in second.

FOXFIRE

It's 1955, and Jeff Chandler
is still a handsome gray
poodle of a man, and Jane Russell's
breasts remain what the slobbering
god of testosterone declared
miraculous, or close enough
to drive Howard Hughes
a cantilevered bra to decree,
which was his way of falling
deeply in love, before he skulked
completely out of reach and got
a crush on his own toenails.
                              OK,
it's not 1955, though all three
of the aforesaid would be better off,
not to mention my father, my mother,
and my best friend, Barry,
who were not dead then. Actually
it's 1991, not that long ago

yet, and I'm home for lunch
from my job as a teacher,
which, in 1955,
I'd have ranked below salesman,
and I'm watching a 1955
movie, a romance entitled *Foxfire,*
on our kitchen TV. But
something about the way Chandler
and Russell glide so cozily among
the grayish trees and bungalows
shifts me back to Omaha about
midway through one of the many
afternoons I spent in my room
building plastic model airplanes,
this particular day with my father
watching the Bears and Cardinals,
—*Chicago* Cardinals—and my mother
folding underwear in the basement,
and Doris Day massaging the last
bar of "Secret Love" from my bedside

Crosley, and my best friend, who
became a doctor brilliant enough
to have healed many of his now
fellow dead, just finished
with the lawn and ready for me
to phone about declaring another
dirt clod war at the house
going up on 87th, he
who I sometimes dream is home
again with a one-in-five chance.

On all those afternoons, including
this one, which happened to be
hot and windy, I loved the scent
of my Testor's Extra Fast Drying
Model Airplane Glue when I
daubed it along a wing assembly
or whatever, not understanding
such chemistry till much
later, loved it enough so that,

due to the sometimes simultaneity
of her singing and the gluing,
and for what might have been
about a year, I was crazy
for Doris Day, who, though
my loyalty would have amazed her,
went on to love only dogs,
and not the Jeff Chandler kind.

So, what besides
model airplane glue
kept me in my room so much
in those Ozzie and Harriet days?
I'll tell you: my family wasn't
what you'd call the Nelsons, but,
then, neither were the Nelsons
—the same way it's not 1955,
or even 1991,
now or then
or ever.

ENCOUNTER AT AN
OUT-OF-TOWN BAR

So here we stand, crossed up in time's unfunny
funhouse, exclaiming, shaking hands. It's Greg,
my buddy-from-the-old-neighborhood's big brother,
ten years old when I was eight, too big
to hang around with us, though he beat up guys
who beat us up, beat up *us* one time,
though just a little, to keep things in proportion.
Anyway, here we sit now, shaking heads
at such coincidence, ordering a beer, starting
to swap outlines of where we've been since vanishing
from Pierce Street forty years ago. It's exotic,
though the facts prove homely (he's a union rep,
I teach college, he's divorced, I'm not,
our youngest kids are nearly grown) and the jolt
from how we were to how we are brings
to mind some fifties horror flick in which
the victims, tagged with the mummy's curse or the goo
from outer space, have just this moment
found each other's svelte good looks

bloated, bleached, shrunk, wrinkled, and rendered
nearly bald. It's their cue to scream like hell
and try to run away, though each one looks
as scary as the next.
                  Whether Greg's distracted too,
the chat falters, the beer takes on a rusty
aftertaste, till we can't stand our lucky
meeting anymore, agreeing we'll have to
look each other up, hurrying outside
to the eyes of strangers, the routine light of day.

DOCTOR'S APPOINTMENT

We sit along the walls,
as snowfluffs float past windows.
The afternoon a loss, we're resigned
to a day or two of trots
and fever—except the man
across from me, who's wearing
slippers. His mind's on something
else. It almost shows
beneath the waxy face, tight
as a surgeon's glove, the grieving
eyes that scan from floor
to folded hands and back,
the oily, tufted pate.

He's had to bring it here,
to this pastel lounge
for baby sneezes and politely
silent farts, to crowd the sitter
next to him, who turns

slightly away and slumps deeper
into last month's *Field
and Stream.* On the other
side his wife clutches
a heavy purse, her legs
planted wide as a cornerback's.

He sighs, leans forward
like someone listening for voices
from another room and hearing
only the seashell whispers
of his inner ear. I settle
back, try not to stare.
Behind a bookcase,
someone's child bangs out
the scales on a toy piano.
"Every good boy does fine,"
spouts memory, smug
as a teacher's pet. "Every
good boy does fine."

AT MY WIFE'S FAMILY REUNION

Twenty years and still an alien from the planet
of claustrophobic families who can't wait
not to see each other, whatever the occasion,
I'm caught once more in this press of in-laws,
who every year clank out the folding chairs
on the tiles of Fellowship Hall and line them up
before the folding tables, the middle two
of which will bear the covered dishes.

"Hi," I flinch, edging away, "Good
to see you," as the gene pool laps and tows
and sunstreaks heat the ancient scent
of Bible school. This year's babies gaze
through the news: Cousin Thelma's latest flaunting
—the one at the Purple Heart Motel, the one
that made the paper—and always the vast necrology
steady as Uncle Harry's liver cancer.

Harry sits at a corner table with Aunt Joyce,
his meal untouched, receiving comforters, agreeing

that the price of hail insurance is a crime. His son,
wobbly from a morning toot, snaps the memorial
picture. After cake, flashbulbs go off
wild as at a premier. And Harry, in fact,
seems comforted, at home as a brittle leaf
on a red-orange maple, ready for a quiet fall.

At dusk we caravan past Autumn House
to the family plot, long run out of space,
the last two stones awaiting only
final dates. After prayer, Harry
stands like a cliff diver calculating depths
as respects are paid and groups begin their separate
departures to another Monday. My wife lingers
in the settling silence. I lean on the car and wait,
hearing nothing above the breath of pines
and a mower droning steadily in the distance.

BREAK

As the waves fade before the inbound darkness,
lights behind the beach switch on, igniting
the crests, highlighting the few souls still
out on the chilly sand. Seated with my wine
at the corner of the restaurant's ocean view,
I watch a man and a woman, Chicano and Anglo,
build a campfire slowly, at their leisure,
like Adam and Eve on the first, easy night.
She removes her sandals as he adds a stick
of wood, then pops the first Bud from their cooler.
My watch says 8. I'll give myself two hours
on this glassed-in shore, my back to where
my father worries the restraining strap,
then drifts out to try death's door again,
while Mother carries on, her grief long
ground down to the roots, all the nerves
gone black. "Just look!" she said, hoisting
his arm as she might a sleeve from the laundry basket,
his flesh sagging from the bone where I once

perched for a snapshot in his service cap. Signs
all over town cheered WELCOME HOME and WELL DONE,
the foe routed. He spits his food back now,
thrusting out his tongue like a bayonet
he wants to shove in us, the benighted living,
trying to tempt him back with applesauce.
The doctor's clipped a sign to his door: "No
IV feeding, No CPR."

                  Waiting on the main course,
I watch the waves file in one by one, let them wash
my eyes, my hands. The campfire's ready for the franks,
though the couple chats on, taking in the night.

PHANTOM SLEEP

The sandman's haymaker, nada's
Sunday roundhouse, oblivion's
bolo punch, it gives memory
the slip when, sleepless at 4 A.M.,
you kick the clammy sheet off,
wondering if you've slept
your last, if in a week or so
the state will come with straps
and rubber gloves to coax you
to a room devised for shadow boxing
round the clock, but then,
from the bird cries and that slash of light
across your legs, you realize it's really
sunrise, though even now
—if now it is instead of meanwhile
or once upon a time—you're not
quite sure you know the count, sprawled
there blinking like some club palooka
paid to test the contender's new

left hook, your head a lava lamp
of sludgy notions: you need more
roadwork, a longer reach, someone
in your corner. Say your name. What's
your name? How many fingers?

URN BURIAL

Only the cheap one is vase-shaped,
topaz clay stamped with the Praying Hands,
something they might have buried Elvis in
if he'd played it safe and stuck with trucking.

The rest are boxes, mahogany to bronze,
marked with a cross or the face of Jesus, or
just a tree or flower. One size fits all
adults, two smaller ones for youngsters.

Not much, finally, to choose from, for the one
who's playing Daddy today, making the big
decisions. So, Dad, it's the flower or the tree,
though you might have claimed something churchier.

The tree, I think, a weeping willow
(Christ!) cut deep into an antiqued bronze
container all too reminiscent of the Popeye
jack-in-the-box I once bought for your birthday.

But it's not so bad, a good willow likeness,
nothing crass or holier than thou,
just a tree that seems to sigh more than weep,
privately, peacefully, at long last.

MISSING PERSON

In a closet box of photos: sixteen color slides,
labeled "December '56," of our Omaha backyard,
snow-patched, the sky cast iron, trees slight
and unlovely as bundled Christmas switches.
A view from the picture window. Sixteen times.
"Dad loved that house," my sister explained.

So. I begin with a new-bought house in winter,
a snowscape shot by a man for whom photography,
all art, was rouge and powder. Or should I begin
with the camera, that snazzy Leica he captured
back in Germany, where he sported moustache
and shoulder holster. Or was it simply
the snow that day, or something else that day
that made the snow play chords so willowy
and sweet he just kept shooting—soldier
of the bottom line, trying to catch the light
just so, beside himself with something
he couldn't name, would never think to mention.

FIRST BIRD OF SPRING

I can't say why it is, except it's the first
I've noticed on this first warm day since fall,
couldn't even say what kind it is
though it's too big to be a chickadee
and colored too much like a chickadee
to be a robin. Anyway, it's fat
and unafraid, eyeing me now and then
from the bush outside our kitchen window,
though mostly it surveys, as if it owned the place,
bush, lawn, house, and deferential
evergreens, its folded wings so like
a morning coat, its tufted breast an ascot.

So here we are, two creatures celebrating
spring the way it's usually done, no speech
or bacchanal or marching bands: just
standing there taking in the change,
till sunlight flows into the room from behind the moving
clouds and ignites the faucet into gold

that nearly blinds. It's a cue for His Birdness to blossom
into song, but when my eyes recover,
nothing's on that branch, which quivers now
as if inviting me to take my turn
while the light goes down and a fanfare rumbles in the distance.

LIVING WITH SOLAR KERATOSIS

I do not think that they will sing for me.

While I watch my son flail out beyond my call
on the Boogie board we rented, everything
goes California—big blue swells cresting white,
beach blankets, beach games, beach sun,
beach flies—and here I stand, like a scarecrow
blown in from some prairie, dressed for fall
in hat and jacket, a red towel draped
over my head, nose painted white,
arms waving at the world's largest ocean.

I'm everybody's parent, who's always there
to haggle down delight: slurp that Coke
before you wipe its mouth off and, bang,
it's herpes-A; swim right after snacking,
and you sleep with the fish; play too long
in sunshine, and you're the poster child
for Dermatology Week. That man on Fourth Street?
Remember him? The one with half an ear,
who pulls the little wagon? I'll count to *three!*

The boys are spiking volleyballs; girls in strings
jiggle by. I need a drink in the darkness
of that dive across the street, but my son
needs me here. Everybody needs me here,
dour ant to chaperon the giddy hoppers,
memento mori on the tube of Coppertone,
a blinking light among the pleasure craft,
sometimes tittered at, though underneath
a surprisingly fun guy, a Beach Boys fan.

SOMETIMES ON THE PORCH
IN SUMMER

As the sun begins to settle down for dusk
and the Methodist Church carillon nags again
toward the final bars of "Oh, My Soul,"
two cicadas tune up overhead in the maple
that started shoulder high to our oldest
and now shades half the house till noon.
It's too late for new business, too early
for the nightly bacchanal at the frat house
down the street. The neighborhood's on pause,
and so are we, waiting for another page
to turn, for our youngest to get back
from his paper route, for the roast to cook.

One cicada tries a few fast licks,
the other answers, then there's almost silence:
a radio plays from the pink apartment house
that blocks our view, a pickup rumbles past,
a dog barks in the distance. For a moment,
time falters, the great gears disengage,

and nearly every yard becomes angelic
in this hush of deepening green, where sprinklers
catch the evening light and toss it back,
where the nighthawks tuck their wings and plunge.

MOWING THE LAWN

Dripping sweat, I rotate toward a patch
I missed, intent on unanimity. I want
things level, if only here, if only
for tonight. I want my ducks lined up,
the wrinkles out, the bubble square on plumb
—everything consistent as the lawns
around Versailles or the eighteenth green
at Pebble Beach. Hospital corners.
Sanitary strips. But, while the sun bows out
at the proper angle, some swallows liquored up
on autumn air swoop and veer, playing
chicken with the fence, the trees, my legs,
to pepper up the chase. "Delight," they scrawl.
"Ned loves Molly," "Betty Sue + Paul."

FALL WEATHER

Settled on the porch,
I salute this evening
front from Canada, the first
since June, with a glass
of Napa Valley's finest
and watch the west
go orange and oranger
still—when a girl appears
down the block,
a blonde in shorts,
pumping an apple-colored
ten-speed up the sidewalk;
or maybe it's a woman burning
calories or bridges: she's
moving too fast for me
to see much more
than her card-shark's grin
and, beneath her light
green blouse, breasts that point

and bob in unison, left
then right, synchronized
with knees, while she talks
to herself, a low pep talk,
or, I can't tell, sings
to herself, a fight song,
closing fast in a film
of spokes and shins
and ticking sprockets.
I'm standing now,
staring as she sweeps
in like a dancer fanned
in strobe lights or that
Nude, descending another
staircase, her parts
in many more places
than one at once
and gaining speed uphill,
now flashing past

in a sizzle of tires
through the orange
and gray and sloping
green of twilight,
the sprinklers flinging hats
as she drives deeper
into dusk, then drops
behind the hill, leaving me
apple-cheeked and the moon
transparent as a loose coin
spinning on a counter.